DIGITAL PARENTING
BY THE AGES

By Ben Halpert and Jennifer Geller
Savvy Cyber Kids

ISBN: 978-0-9827968-7-0

Contents

Introduction

Growing up in a digital world, our children are adopting technologies—touching, seeing and interacting with them, and ultimately, understanding the world through the lens of these tools—at younger ages and faster rates than ever before. As a parent, it's worthwhile to pause and think about what this means for children at all ages, considering everything from brain development to socialization, physical safety and, of course, cyber ethics and cyber safety.

* * *

There was a time when the childhood lessons of "don't talk to strangers," and the "golden rule" were enough to keep kids safe. These lessons could be applied to more mature circumstances as the child aged and because kids learned them young, they were better equipped to make safe decisions when they got older. But times have changed. Technology happened. Today, kids have unfettered access to internet-enabled screens, likened to taking the front door off the family home and inviting strangers—potentially dangerous ones—in to play.

Parenting has never been easy. But parenting in the Digital Age has brought with it new challenges that must be addressed to ensure the health and well-being of our kids. The mistakes our children can make—posting something that gets them kicked off a team or refused entry to the college of their choice or connecting with a child predator who grooms them over time—has the potential to haunt them for the rest of their lives, or worse yet, put them in a life or death situation.

The reality is that there is no one-stop prescriptive formula for keeping kids safe online. Technology changes very quickly, so the approach of merely advising on the apps or platforms to use/avoid or specific direction on parental controls is not effective enough. Our children need adults guiding them towards safe and appropriate behavior. They need their parents and caregivers to treat the virtual world like the playground that it is and establish safety protocols early in child development. Parents then must refresh these lessons again and again as the child ages. This is The Tech Talk (don't worry, we will provide you conversation starters!).

Open—then maintain—the lines of communication with your child about all issues related to technology. Your children need to see you as a resource for their online safety when they see something that they don't understand, upsets them or when they make a mistake. Be aware that if you yell at your children or punish them for bringing something to your attention, that may discourage them from confiding in you.

Remember, your children admire and look up to you as their role models. Every day they witness how you interact with technology. If you use your device at meals, they will grow up and use their devices at meals. If you spend all of your free time on social media, they will most likely do the same once they get an account. So be sure to model the behavior you would like to see from them.

* * *

Savvy Cyber Kids offers strategies to parents and educators to provide guidance around appropriate technology usage and to educate children about cyber safety and cyber ethics. This guide, organized by age and grade level, highlights recommendations and learning focus areas that will help you develop appropriate technology practices for your family.

Chapter 1:
Infants and Toddlers

Technology Guidelines

According to the American Academy of Pediatrics (AAP), "children younger than two years need hands-on exploration and social interaction with trusted caregivers to develop their cognitive, language, motor and social emotional skills." There is no substitute—by a screen or digital media of any kind—that can help children in this age group appropriately develop "symbolic, memory and attentional skills" the way that interaction with a caregiver can provide. Human interaction is a road map to the future, a head start for the well-being of the child.

RECOMMENDATIONS

- Children in this age group should have almost no screen time if they are younger than two years old (sorry, no digital babysitters!).
- The only exception is video-chat (like Skype, Google Duo or FaceTime) to allow social connections with distant or traveling relatives. However, be aware that children need parental support to understand what they are seeing.
- The arrival of a new baby is often shared broadly on social media. New parents should determine what information about their children they are comfortable sharing online and with whom.
- By sharing intimate personal information online, parents are teaching children that they are safe in the virtual world. Defining what is private in your family will help your child, as they get older, understand and respect concepts like privacy and security.
- Those precious naked baby bathing pictures and videos you as a parent love and cherish should not be shared on social media. There is no such thing as privacy on social media—even if you think you are limiting who can see your posts, pictures, and videos—there is no way to truly limit who has access to your posts.

Chapter 2:
Preschool through
2nd Grade

Technology Guidelines

The American Academy of Pediatrics has stated that the research advocating for the educational potential of interactive media for young children is limited. As such, their recommendations for technology use for this age group are rooted more heavily by concerns about overuse during this important period of rapid brain development.

While the AAP has cited some research-based evidence of successful learning from high-quality television programs, apps and ebooks, they emphasize that "higher-order thinking skills and executive functions essential for school success, such as task persistence, impulse control, emotion regulation, and creative, flexible thinking," are best taught through hands-on, unstructured and social play.

Parents should also be aware that the AAP warns that overuse and misuse of media at these ages can result in negative impacts—including weight gain later in childhood, reduced sleep quality, and cognitive, language, and social/emotional delays, especially when parent's use a screen as a "distraction from parent-child interactions and child play results in fewer verbal and nonverbal interactions between parents and children."

In addition, the AAP states that all screen time should be WITH an adult and not be used alone. Children do not understand what they are watching or interacting with. This is their first exposure to so many different aspects of life that an adult needs to be with them to explain what they are actually seeing and whether it is positive or negative.

At these ages, really, the moment your child picks up a device and starts playing with a screen, it is time to start The Tech Talk—parent/child conversations about staying safe online. Young children can be taught safety lessons like protecting personal information, understanding who are strangers in the online world (anyone they don't know first in real life), cyberbullying and screen time balance. Remember, once The Tech Talk starts, it never stops.

RECOMMENDATIONS:

- No screens in the bedroom at bedtime. The exception is an e-ink device, such as a Kindle Paperwhite with parental controls set.
- Limit digital media use to 1 hour per day for children 2 to 5 years old. Emphasize hands-on, unstructured and social play.
- Tell your kids to NEVER take pictures or videos of private parts, no matter who asks and despite the fact that they may see celebrities behaving differently. No NUDES—not ever! In most locations, it is illegal to take, send, and even ASK for nudes or sexts of anyone considered a minor.
- Digital media use by young children should be an adult-child shared experience. Parents and caregivers can facilitate the learning process by watching the media with the child and then re-teaching the content to the child.
- Allow children to build secure relationships with caregivers, lessoning the need to rely on screens and digital media for companionship. These relationships should be defined by communication between the child and the caregiver.
- Balance any media use with other healthy activities—including sleep, exercise, play, reading aloud and social interactions, establishing the groundwork for healthy lifelong behaviors.
- Create unplugged spaces and times in the home, including turning off televisions and devices when they are not in use, no screens at mealtimes or in bedrooms at nighttime and curtailing media use an hour before bedtime.
- Don't use media to soothe a child as it can limit a child's ability to self-soothe and regulate emotions.
- Be aware that parent/caregiver technology habits shape how your children grow up using technology.

Technology Concepts & Activities

SAVVY CYBER KIDS RESOURCES:

Savvy Cyber Kids' award-winning children's picture book series, *The Savvy Cyber Kids at Home* for children in preschool through 2nd grade: https://savvycyberkids.org/shop/books-for-children/. You can find free lesson plans and activity sheets that go along with the activities for each book as discussed below at https://savvycyberkids.org/educators/.

ACTIVITIES: BOOK 1

Learning About Computers, Privacy, and Strangers

1. As you read the first Savvy Cyber Kids at Home book, *The Family Gets a Computer*, pause when appropriate and ask your children to describe what computers are and what they do.
2. After reading the book, ask your children to describe vocabulary words:
   - Savvy
   - Computer
   - Safety
   - Online
   - Cyber
   - Personal
3. Model how you can create a safe identity for yourself online—talk about hobbies, interests, favorite shows, favorite colors, etc.
   - Just as the characters in the book created superhero identities to protect themselves when online, ask your children to create their own online secret identity for when they are online why they chose it.
   - Have your children do an art project where the children draw their online secret identity or design a superhero cape that matches their new secret identity.

ACTIVITIES: BOOK 2

Learning About Bullying and Appropriate Response

Read the second book in the Savvy Cyber Kids at Home book series, *Defeat of the Cyberbully*.

1. Ask your children to describe vocabulary words and concepts:
   - Trust
   - Game
   - Team
   - Bully
   - Step Up
   - Personal
2. Ask your children questions:
   - What is a bully?
   - Have you ever been bullied?
   - Have you ever seen anyone else get bullied?
   - If you have been a target of a bully, what did you do? Who did you tell?
   - Discuss the idea of not standing by while someone else is being bullied.
3. Model for your children how you would identify someone who is a trusted adult. Explain some of the traits you would look for in such a person.
   - Facilitate an art project where the children draw (and decorate) two trusted adults (parent, grandparent, aunt, uncle, teacher, etc.).

ACTIVITIES: BOOK 3

Learning About Screen Time and Technology Balance

Read the third book in the *Savvy Cyber Kids at Home* book series, *Adventures Beyond the Screen*.

1. Ask your children to describe vocabulary words:
   - Activity
   - Inside (Indoor)
   - Outside (Outdoor)
   - Screen Time
   - Bored
2. Ask your children questions:
   - What is a screen time?
   - What are screen time/technology limits?
   - What is your favorite book to read?
   - What is your favorite activity to do indoors?
   - What is your favorite activity to do outdoors?
   - What is your favorite movie?
3. Ask about their experiences with limits and how they feel about them.
   - Model for your children making a list with two columns, with one column labeled INSIDE and the other column labeled OUTSIDE. Then list an activity in each column as an example. Have your children create their own two-column list and list at least three activities in each column that they could do if they were not using technology. Once each column has at least three activities in it, have the children order each list separately in order of preference, favorite activity = 1 and least favorite = the highest number of items listed (many children may list more than 3 activities).
   - Ask your children to explain to you their favorite activities and why.

Chapter 3:
3rd through 5th Grade

Technology Guidelines

It's time to delve deeper into the concepts of information and privacy, exploring why they are important and how they can keep you safe in the cyber world.

Explore the concept of a cyber stranger with your child and encourage him/her to see anyone they interact with online—unless they are family or a physical-world friend—as a stranger who should always be treated as a stranger. Discuss how we deal with strangers in the physical world: at a store, at a mall, at a park, on the street, in a car that pulls up, and how that relates to cyber strangers.

Talk your kids about respect, empathy and consent as it relates to decision-making—BEFORE someone else teaches them how not to behave. When interacting online, your kids will be seen in a positive light by others if they understand these concepts.

As your child spends more time online in arenas where they are exposed to strangers, it's time to have an age-appropriate modern-day sex talk, covering consent, compliance, predator grooming, pornography and sexting—**at much younger ages than ever before, in order to help our kids understand what they may be exposed to and family-appropriate ways to respond or react**.

RECOMMENDATIONS:
- No screens in the bedroom at bedtime. The exception is an e-ink device, such as a Kindle Paperwhite with parental controls set.
- Be involved in your children's digital lives, stay aware of their favorite game, app or social media community—including how they interact with these technologies and with who!
- Tell your kids to NEVER take pictures or videos of private parts, no matter who asks and despite the fact that they may see celebrities behaving differently. No NUDES—not ever! In most locations, it is illegal to take, send, and even ASK for nudes or sexts of anyone considered a minor.

- Set technology limits with your children, including screen and screen time and gaming time limits and rules to control when technology is used:
  - Keep devices in a family charging area at night and during play dates.
  - No devices at meal times. (this goes for parents/caregivers too!)
- Use only one screen at a time as research shows that using multiple screens inhibits fine motor skill and other brain development.
- Get your kids to always ask before downloading apps and games—and making in-game purchases! Use technology to help you by restricting the ability to download and purchase items without your permission.
- Discuss online predators as strangers that look to harm kids like them. Emphasize the importance of not texting, talking, video chatting, sending pictures to people you do not know in real life.
- Make a list (and keep it current!) of all your child's user IDs and passwords regularly check on what they are doing to make sure they are safe.
- Talk to your kids about what home technology rules make sense for how you want to raise your child in a world filled with technology. Involve them in the conversation, let them provide input on what they think.

Technology Concepts & Activities

SAVVY CYBER KIDS RESOURCES:

- Use the Savvy Cyber Kids News Feed (https://savvycyberkids.org/tech-talk/savvy-cyber-kids-news-feed/)to be aware of when technology is used for bad and for good. Read it daily to select an article to use as a conversation starter with your child. These teachable moments are happening around the globe every day. We also post conversation starter questions related to these news articles on our Facebook, Instagram, Twitter, and LinkedIn accounts.
- Read Savvy Cyber Kids' Parent's Guide: Let's Talk About Sex (https://savvycyberkids.org/families/) so that you are prepared to help your child navigate what they WILL see online.
- Read Savvy Cyber Kids' Parent's Guide: Who Is A Stranger (https://savvycyberkids.org/families/) so that you can help you child understand why a stranger is ALWAYS a stranger no longer how long you 'know' them online.

ACTIVITIES:

Technology Pledge
Complete the Savvy Cyber Kids Technology Pledge (https://savvycyberkids.org/technology-pledge/) with your child using the set of selectable rules for technology use in your home that will ensure that your child is thinking about cyber ethics, safety, and privacy.

Learning About Cyber Safety and Cyber Ethics
1. Ask your children to describe vocabulary words:
   - Bystander
   - Empathy
   - Respect
   - Troll
   - Stranger
   - Safety
   - Social Media
   - Addiction
   - Password
   - Privacy
   - Chat
   - Gaming
2. Start discussions with your children on topics:
   - Game trash talk and how it can make friends feel
   - Your child's experience witnessing or experiencing cyberbullying
   - The ways to use technology for good
   - How to avoid poor decisions that can lead to trouble
   - What respect for themselves means and how to apply that to respect for others
   - The concept of empathy for others
   - Seeking mental and physical balance between online and offline worlds

Learning About Consent

1. Ask your children to describe vocabulary words:
    *   Safety
    *   Affection
    *   Feelings
    *   Body Language
    *   Boundaries
    *   Permission
    *   Consent
2. Ask your children questions:
    *   What does it mean to give consent?
    *   What does consent sound like?
    *   When do we need to ask for consent?
    *   When can consent be confusing?
    *   What can you do/say if you do not give consent?
    *   Role play with your children to explore the gray areas, like if someone says "yes" but their tone and body language really says "no."

Have Fun with Technology

Use technology to further relationships with family members:

*   Research and try out gaming platforms where parent and child or grandparent and grandchild can interact.
    *   Ancestry websites, like Ancestry.com and MyHeritage.com let you explore family history together.
    *   Read together with Readeo.
    *   Collaborate together on homework with Scoot & Doodle.
    *   Chat with family members using Google Duo or Facetime.
    *   Find online versions of games that 'kids' of all ages can play like Wheel of Fortune.
*   Create emoji puzzles to have a family member solve.

Chapter 4:
6th through 8th Grade

Technology Guidelines

Adolescence is an extremely vulnerable age and technology only magnifies the insecurities, awkwardness and missteps that can happen. Here is a look at what is happening with today's youth:

- The average age for a child getting their first smartphone is 10-years-old.
- 64% of kids have access to the internet via their own devices.
- 39% of kids get a social media account at 11-years-old.
- The average age kids first see pornography consistently lands at between seven and eleven-years-old.

By middle school, most kids have a cell phone and a window into a world of trouble. Born into a world surrounded in every possible way by technology, pre-teens and teens are inevitably drawn to their phones. The places they can go, the people they can meet—and yes, the dangers they can get into, all from the safety of their homes and schools are limitless. That's a lot of responsibility and sometimes it's not that easy to make the right choice or understand potential consequences behind a screen, with abundant seemingly gray areas to navigate.

As your child becomes more immersed in their digital worlds, from gaming to social media platforms, continue to have discussions that encourage them to use respect and empathy with online interactions. Reinforce the need to always question what they see online and seek adult advice to assess the authenticity and safeness of what they are experiencing.

Show your children how to take charge of their online privacy and image, from setting social media platforms to private, understanding the limitations of privacy settings, recognizing the need for appropriate online behaviors, to how to respond to negative interactions online—with persistent strangers or cyber bullies, and the permanence of their online identity and its impact on obtaining an internship, getting into a college, getting a job, and keeping a job.

There is an unknown—and potentially dark—side to technology. Your child's brain is still developing and constant exposure to screens will quite literally wire their brain in ways different than previous generations. While much is unknown about the long-term impact of growing up in The Digital Age, experts are expressing pointed concerns about young people's ability to focus and to be imaginative. If attention is the gateway to thinking—and fast-paced, shallow media is what youth consume—it makes sense that information overload leads to poor decision-making, memory and learning. The result will be a generation of thinkers and doers who are radically different than those who came before them.

Technology use, especially technology overuse, including social media and gaming, has shown to exacerbate many issues a child may have. Sadness, loneliness, anxiety, depression, and addictive behaviors are unfortunately brought to the forefront when a balance between life with and without technology is not maintained.

As a digital parent, you have the ability to provide a counter-acting influence on how technology affects your child. It's not about saying no to technology. It's about also placing a high value on screen time moderation, on adventures off the screen and being sure, in subtle—and maybe not so subtle—ways that your child also experiences the world off of a screen. This commitment will undoubtedly benefit your child for years to come.

RECOMMENDATIONS:

- No screens in the bedroom at bedtime. The exception is an e-ink device, such as a Kindle Paperwhite with parental controls set.
- When it comes to gaming, research parental controls for each game and gaming platform to suit your family's need for privacy and security.
- Make sure your kids understand that accounts, profile settings, user names, gamer tags and the like should not include any personal information—including name, gender, where you live or go to school.
- Tell your kids to NEVER take pictures or videos of private parts, no matter who asks and despite the fact that they may see celebrities behaving differently. No NUDES—not ever! In most locations, it is illegal to take, send, and even ASK for nudes or sexts of anyone considered a minor.
- Make sure your children understand that they should always ask before taking someone's picture or making a video—and to get permission before sharing images of others online.
- Teach your children not to over-share online—including what they are doing and when. It is best to share moments after the event has occurred, not during.
- Emphasize the importance of empathy and encourage your kids to only post and share nice things. Make sure your child understands that texting, communication apps, online forums, and social media are unacceptable places to argue or to try and resolve conflicts with peers.
- Recognize that too much screen time may have a negative impact on your child's development and make sure that how they experience the world is not exclusively via a screen.

- Establish—and stick to—technology-free zones and time periods to help your child be comfortable both on and offline. These limits apply to ALL household members!
- Talk to your kids about having a positive self body image and why they think other kids may use apps to change their appearance online. Model the behavior you wish to see in your children's technology use.
- Your children are exposed to pornography, and in most cases extreme hardcore pornography, at a very young age. Talk to your children about relationships and your family's expectations on how to treat others.

Technology Concepts & Activities

SAVVY CYBER KIDS RESOURCES:
- Complete the Savvy Cyber Kids Technology Pledge (https://savvycyberkids. org/technology-pledge/), a set of selectable rules for technology use in your home that will ensure that your child is thinking about cyber ethics, safety, and privacy.
- Read Savvy Cyber Kids' Parent's Guide To Gaming (https://savvycyberkids. org/families/) so that you can help your child game safely.
- Read Savvy Cyber Kids' Parent's Guide: Let's Talk About Sex (https:// savvycyberkids.org/families/) and start talking to your child about sex.

ACTIVITIES:

Technology Pledge
Complete the Savvy Cyber Kids Technology Pledge (https://savvycyberkids. org/technology-pledge/) with your child using the set of selectable rules for technology use in your home that will ensure that your child is thinking about cyber ethics, safety, and privacy.

Stop. Think. Connect.
1. At this age, your child has to make their own decisions about appropriate behavior online. Every action they take will follow a decision they make. You need to give your children the critical thinking skills to pause, or stop for a moment—when they are about to post on social media or take any action online—then have them think about the following questions:
    - How would I feel if someone posted this about me?
    - What will people think of me?
    - What will people think of the other person?
    - Is this the right thing to do?

2. Use the Savvy Cyber Kids News Feed (https://savvycyberkids.org/tech-talk/savvy-cyber-kids-news-feed/) as conversation starters with your teen to find examples of when teens made poor decisions with technology and ask your child where mistakes were made and why.
3. Continue the dialogue about making these kinds of decisions by asking your child:
    *   Have you ever seen anything online or in a game that made you feel uncomfortable?
    *   Has anyone said anything strange or inappropriate to you in an app or game?
    *   Has anything online has made you feel uncomfortable, hurt their feelings or confused them?
4. Let your child know you are always available to help them understand what they are experiencing as they enjoy the benefits of having technology in their lives.

What Is Private?

1. As a family, discuss the idea of privacy. From the youngest ages, children must understand that they should never share their real name and their physical or email address and phone number. Once your children understand basic privacy concepts, take the discussion to the next level. Young people need to understand that they shouldn't be sharing the name of the school that they go to—even by wearing a school shirt in a profile picture, where they take after-school activities, family routines or whether Mom and Dad are home or away, with anyone that isn't a friend in the physical world.
2. Discuss the different technologies that the family uses. Determine which use location tracking—including photos on your child's phone—and how to minimize access to your location by adjusting settings.
3. Teens of this generation have a different opinion about what should be private and what is private. Is a text private? A group chat? Apps and features that claim to be private? Our kids trust their friends but do they know how to tell if a friend is trustworthy and do they understand the ways that any communication can betray their privacy. Debunk the myth of privacy in the virtual world. It 100% doesn't exist and your kids need to know that.

Who Is A Stranger?

1. Ask your children if they have ever received a message from someone in a game or app that they don't know in the physical world. Explain to your kids that the physical world includes your home, friends they play with in your neighborhood, at school, on sports teams and through other extra-curricular activities. Discuss how you can't definitively know who a person is if they are not known to you from the physical world. They may be misrepresenting themselves and they may not be safe to engage with. Teach your child to see strangers as strangers. No amount of nice things they say or gifts that they send can change the fact that these people are strangers.

2. Make sure your kids understand that they should never meet someone they met online, through an app, game, or social media community in the physical world. Not ever.

3. The ways young people make social connections are different than generations before. Your children have access to friends of friends—many of whom they may not have met in-person. Your child may explain to you that their friend wants them to become online friends with others because of shared interests. The danger is that your child may not know—and you will not know—if this new friend is an IRL (in real life) friend of your child's friend—and if this person is even who they say they are!

4. Ask your child for examples of friends/followers and gamers that they interact with, how they made the connection, how they interact, and what information they have shared in the past.

5. Define your family's rules for 'friend-making'. For older children, it may be useful to distinguish the variance in ways that your child can connect online with others. Know that the very act of having this conversation—and continuing to have this conversation as your child gets older—will ensure that you understand your child's online interactions (no matter what new technologies launch) and that your child hears your concerns and is aware of the pitfalls of behaving recklessly in the virtual world.

Building The Critical Thinking Skills in The Age of Fake News

1. These days it's easy to come face-to-face with videos, articles, blog posts and websites that look real and feel authentic, but are fake or at least distorted. Encourage your teen to seek out information that distinguishes fact from opinions, rumors, and lies.

2. With your teen, identify examples of fake news that if believed create the opportunity to be controlled by those who seek to color information to promote their own point of view or agenda.

3. Encourage your teen to ask questions. The goal here is to teach children to question what they read or hear. With older children, talk about sources of information:
   • Is it a reliable news source or a tabloid, a personal blog or a lobbying website?
   • Did they hear it from a classmate who has only heard it from someone else?

4. Make thinking a family affair. Use family time—during mealtimes, on long car rides, or while on trips—to encourage questions and problem-solving techniques. Find a topic that interests your child, cultivate it and encourage them to read books, watch movies and research the topic.

5. Talk about responsibility and consequences. Start a discussion about why sharing news on social media and elsewhere online may not be a good idea, can be polarizing and can have negative consequences. Remind them of the importance of not confusing their own opinions with fact and to pause before automatically sharing information online, before verifying its validity.

Read Together & Further Your Child's Reading Comprehension

As the song goes, 'what the world needs now'...is critical thinking, the objective analysis and evaluation of an issue or information in order to form a judgment. A lot of what we read and see online is distorted—but it's not hard to end up believing something that is not exactly true. How many times have you seen statements as fact, when it is actually opinion or poorly-researched information? It happens all the time, right?

- Engage with them about what they are reading and ask questions. Give your children the opportunity to think actively, not passively, as they read.
- Talk about passages or plots that are challenging to them and help them figure out how they can gain knowledge to understand difficult concepts.
- Ask them to make connections in what they are reading, predicting how a story might end or making a comparison to something in real life.
- Invite them to summarize a section of a book or an entire story to identify the important themes. This can help you see what they do and don't understand. You can also read newspaper articles and check facts together to show them how to use analytical and critical thinking skills.

How To Game With Strangers

If your child is a fan of multiplayer online games, and you're wondering how to keep them safe without stinting their fun, here's what you need to be sure that they know:

- Their gamer tag should not reveal their name, age, or gender. They should never reveal where they live or what school they go to. Email addresses, phone numbers, photos of their face, and gaming account passwords are also off-limits.
- Your child should understand that they should never accept an invitation to communicate with another gamer they do not know on a non-gaming platform or app. Remind your child that a stranger is ALWAYS a stranger, even when online interactions may make them seem familiar.
- In the online world, you never truly know who is behind the screen. Your child should never, EVER agree to meet up with a stranger offline.
- Even as the intensity builds in a game, always remind your child to communicate with respect and empathy towards fellow players.

Sleeping with Your Devices

Experts agree that sleeping with devices distracts adolescents, lessens their hours of much-needed rest and alters their natural circadian system. Research the circadian system, and how it controls our natural sense of time, and the impacts of sleep deprivation with your teen. Talk about how notifications and the blue light projected from mobile devices alters this system, disrupting your teen's senses, meaning he/she will not receive a full eight hours of undisturbed sleep. Explain to your teen that they would not choose to be constantly physically with their friends in real life, so logically they should not be constantly virtually with their friends. Ask your child questions:

- Why do you think it may not be the best idea to be connected to your friends at all times?
- Why do you think having devices with screens near you at night disturbs your sleep?
- How much sleep does your brain need at your current age? How about me?

"Disappearing" Photos

It's time to debunk the myth that photos can be kept private. Explain to your teen that nothing put online can really be deleted. It can all be traced back to you—and later revealed to embarrassment or worse—causing you to lose access to jobs, teams, schools and jobs. Be sure that before allowing your teen to access apps such as Snapchat, Instagram, or other apps to purport to be a secure way of sending photos, videos, and messages it is important to let your teen know that nothing actually disappears. To bring this message home:

- Ask your teen to do some research on their own to learn how social media companies, device manufacturers', and app developers store all information and why.
- Ask your teen to Google him/herself online and see what they and others can easily learn about your teen.
- Also ask your teen to search for him/herself in various social media apps and see what they find about themselves.

Sexting/The Tech Sex Talk

Parents should recognize that easy access to devices (and the internet) enables teens to see hard-core pornography at earlier and earlier ages. This means that the internet is giving pre-teens and adolescents lessons on sex they may not have received from their parents. Inevitably this access to inappropriate pornographic material can alter an adolescents' morals or their understanding of appropriate relationship and sexual behavior. Ask your teen:

- To explain the meanings of consent, compliance and exploitation and how they relate to [online] sexual activities.
- To explain why sexting is risky and illegal.
- To talk about their understanding of intimate relationships and the characteristics that make for a stronger relationship.

Chapter 5:
9th through 12th Grade

Technology Guidelines

Truth is, before parents know it, upper elementary and middle school turns into high school and beyond and with each passing year, your child will be closer to venturing out on their own. With that freedom comes all the rights AND the responsibilities of independent living. As parents and teachers, we are doing teens a disservice to not prepare them for the complexities of life—particularly the complexities of making smart decisions using all the technology they love.

By now, you may have already covered with your child most of the basics of cyber safety and cyber ethics. And, your child has likely surpassed your tech savviness by leaps and bounds. But just because they know the latest tricks, apps and platforms does not mean that they have internalized how to behave appropriately online. Now is the time to take a deeper dive on the topics previously covered, lifting the veil of protection and showing them just how very false and dangerous their online worlds can be.

If you are just now starting to have The Tech Talk with your older child— it's not too late! They need your guidance now so that they are aware of the challenges that await them.

NOTE: As your child approaches senior year and prepares to head off to college, or moving out to start living on their own, the rules need to change in your home to prepare your child for independent life.

Make sure that your teen understands that making a good impression as an applicant to college or as a job seeker is not merely based on transcripts, resume, recommendations and how you present yourself in an interview. Like it or not, their online persona, also sometimes referred to as a digital footprint, has been crafted via likes, comments, group affiliations and posts.

Your teen should know that when someone is evaluating them, a great deal can be learned from social media profiles, maybe more than your teen would like! Impress upon your teen that they should not let careless social media hygiene keep them from an opportunity that you have been working towards.

RECOMMENDATIONS:

- No screens in the bedroom at bedtime. The exception is an e-ink device, such as a Kindle Paperwhite with parental controls set, until roughly Junior year (see next bullet).
- Once your high schooler has attained the SAT/ACT test score and/or been accepted to the University they will be attending (or is not attending collage but will soon be living on their own), it is time to let the screens back in their bedrooms. You need to help guide your child on how to manage the distractive nature of all screens have to offer and still be able to function the following day. You don't want you child failing out of school first semester because they were gaming all night or on social media at all hours, do you?
- Knowing that teens spend an enormous amount of time cultivating a perfected version of their lives on their social media platforms, spend time talking to your child about the 'real' vs 'virtual' you and the dangers of comparison.
- Teach your child the value of not always being 'connected' and how to seek out and create adventures off the screen.
- Explore with your high schooler how he/she is the curator of their own online identity—that every selfie, every post and every comment shapes how others view them and becomes a resume from which they are judged in the short-term and well-beyond.
- Help your child dissect the false concept of online privacy and anonymity, examining the technologies behind what happens with all the data created on a device and how anything created with technology can always be tracked back to the creator and how nothing is truly private.
- Directly address the dangers of the virtual world and explicitly show your child the vulnerability of young people connecting with strangers online and the seemingly harmless ways predators target young victims.
- Use real-world examples to speak directly to the dangers of typical teen online behavior and encourage your child to use the critical thinking skills they apply in their academics to their experiences in the virtual world.
- Have discussions about using technology, such as social media or dating apps, to meet strangers. While this guide is meant to be assistance when raising children, you can find more information on precautions to take when meeting strangers as young adults on https://savvycyberkids.org/.
- Encourage your teen to maintain their digital persona that is aligned with future goals, like college and a career.

Technology Tech Talk Conversations

SAVVY CYBER KIDS RESOURCES:

- The Savvy Cyber Kids News Feed (https://savvycyberkids.org/tech-talk/savvy-cyber-kids-news-feed/) gathers both the good and the bad news about cyber safety and cyber ethic issues from across the globe, in a weekly email of the headlines and links. Use these articles as conversation starters with your teen.
- Have your teen complete the Savvy Cyber Kids Digital Bill of Rights (https://savvycyberkids.org/digital-bill-of-rights/) and share the results in your profiles so others know how you expect to be treated, and, in turn, how you will treat others.

ACTIVITIES:

Sleeping with Your Devices

Experts agree that sleeping with devices distracts adolescents, lessens their hours of much-needed rest and alters their natural circadian system. Research the circadian system, and how it controls our natural sense of time, and the impacts of sleep deprivation with your teen. Talk about how notifications and the blue light projected from mobile devices alters this system, disrupting your teen's senses, meaning he/she will not receive a full eight hours of undisturbed sleep. Explain to your teen that they would not choose to be constantly physically with their friends in real life, so logically they should not be constantly virtually with their friends. Ask your child questions:

- Why do you think it may not be the best idea to be connected to your friends at all times?
- Why do you think having devices with screens near you at night disturbs your sleep?
- How much sleep does your brain need at your current age? How about me?

Maintaining Privacy Online

Your teen needs to understand that their profile settings, complete with name and other information such as profile picture, is easily found online and is like a key for identity thieves to steal private information and potentially let others track their actions. Talk to your teen about what they can do with every account to maintain their privacy. Whether it's a social media platform or a gaming profile ask your teen why it's important that they take the precautions below:

- Have private accounts if personal information is shared.
- Have public accounts that mask identity and personal information.
- Only accept friends/followers on private accounts that are known in real life.
- Don't reveal private information in social media handles and bios.
- Have passwords that are difficult to guess with varieties of letters/numbers.
- Use two-factor (also called strong) authentication.

- Choose profile names that do not easily identify you.
- Guard your social security number (**the only site that would need that are banking sites when applying of a loan or trying to open up financial accounts**).
- Keep all the software on your device up to date with security updates.
- Make sure all computers (yes, PCs AND Macs) are running anti-virus software.
- Properly dispose (shred) all private information (credit reports, bank statements, receipts).

Assuring You Are Careful with What You Post

1. Teens often feel invincible and don't see past an immediate moment. They need to understand that what they post, snap, comment, tweet, dm, can all come back to haunt them. Explain to your teen that college recruiters and future employers have the resources to track digital histories and see what your teen has posted, commented on and done in video and photo records. Teach your child that who they are online is a representation of who they are and what they stand for. It is important for teens to know that their online profile is often someone's first impression of them. Hence, they should act accordingly. Ask your teen what they think is private online and then have a conversation that may likely challenge their assumptions. They should understand that:
   - What you put out using a device is always traceable.
   - Pressing "delete" does not mean it is erased.
   - Nothing "just goes away."
2. Suggest a litmus test before they post, such as "The Grandparent Rule:" Would I show this photo to my grandpa? Would I let my grandma read this?"

Maintaining Netiquette

1. Though internet-based technologies make it feel like we are face-to-face with everyone at all times, we really are not. While face-to-face interactions are influenced by facial expressions, body cues and social cues, societal expectations and manners, online, these influences are absent and it's easy to take things too far or forget what behaving appropriately means. Your teen needs to implicitly recognize that everything online can be traced back to them, so it is important to always maintain netiquette. Parents should recognize that adolescents learn through example and that digital parenting requires parents to set an example for your teen on how they should act online and treat other people. Ask your teen:
   - To give examples of how online statements can easily be misinterpreted because there is no expression/social cues online.
   - Why deleting a regrettable post may not be effective enough and to explain why they need to be careful about what they post.
   - To give examples of careless or thoughtless posts that could hurt sometimes, because whoever they are communicating with has real feelings.

2. Work with your teen to adopt guidelines and rules for their online interactions:
   - Do not degrade yourself online.
   - Make your digital identity a positive representation of who you.
   - Respect people's privacy.
   - Use the concepts of respect and empathy towards others when thinking about what to post.

Meeting Strangers

1. Probably the most important lesson you want to impart to your teen is that they should never, EVER, meet people in real life who they first met online. Your teen should understand that an online friend of a friend does not equal a friend (someone you know in real-life) because criminals, rapists, pedophiles and others looking to cause them harm are able to infiltrate friend's accounts and then appear to be a "safer" stranger. Remind your teen that this applies to celebrity and influencer accounts—as they are often managed by teams of other people whose true character and intent will remain unknown. Your teen, and the rest of their generation, has different standards on how they make and define friends. It is important to stress to your teen that it is impossible to completely trust someone met online and that people have alter-egos.
   - Ask your teen to explain in their own words why you can never tell if someone is who they say they are, so be safe and don't meet people met online in real life.
   - Ask your teen to give examples of online 'friends' that they have or their friends have that are, in reality, strangers.
   - Ask your teen to describe scenarios where meeting up with an online friend could be suggested so that they recognize it when it is suggested to them and know how to navigate the situation.
2. Work with your teen to define how they should go about "friend-making" online:
   - Use some of the unfortunate examples from the weekly cyber ethics news feed to show how those that wish to cause us harm do so by social engineering us into trusting them and the disastrous result can be life-changing or life-ending.
   - If your child chooses to engage in conversations with someone they never net in the physical world, have them understand the importance of not providing their true information (such as where they live, their phone number, the school they attend, where they work, etc.).

"Disappearing" Photos

It's time to debunk the myth that photos can be kept private. Explain to your teen that nothing put online can really be deleted. It can all be traced back to you—and later revealed to embarrassment or worse—causing you to lose access to jobs, teams, schools and jobs. Be sure that before allowing your teen to access apps such as Snapchat, Instagram, or other apps to purport to be a secure way of sending photos, videos, and messages it is important to let your teen know that nothing actually disappears. To bring this message home:

- Ask your teen to do some research on their own to learn how social media companies, device manufacturers', and app developers store all information and why.
- Ask your teen to Google him/herself online and see what they and others can easily learn about your teen.
- Also ask your teen to search for him/herself in various social media apps and see what they find about themselves.

Sexting/The Tech Sex Talk

Parents should recognize that easy access to devices (and the internet) enables teens to see hard-core pornography at earlier and earlier ages. This means that the internet is giving pre-teens and adolescents lessons on sex they may not have received from their parents. Inevitably this access to inappropriate pornographic material can alter an adolescents' morals or their understanding of appropriate relationship and sexual behavior. Ask your teen:

- To explain the meanings of consent, compliance and exploitation and how they relate to [online] sexual activities.
- To explain why sexting is risky and illegal.
- To talk about their understanding of intimate relationships and the characteristics that make for a stronger relationship.

Cyberbullying

Parents can make sure that their teen is aware of what behaviors are defined as cyberbullying, including hurtful texts, videos, posts, snaps, and comments. Make sure that your teen understands that even though online activities feel anonymous, and therefore, not personal or important, cyberbullying can lead to serious outcomes like depression, low self-esteem, suicidal thoughts and in-school violence. Teach your teen how to recognize cyberbullying and let them know that they should always come directly to you or another adult if something arises. Ask your teen:

- To think through every post, comment and share—thinking about more than just the potential for good (humor, connection) and instead about the potential for harm to others.
- What their experiences have been witnessing or participating in cyberbullying, or being cyberbullied themselves. Talk about how to respond to cyberbullying. If your child is being cyberbullied or is supporting someone who is, encourage them to keep evidence of the communications (it is okay to save chats or screenshot).

Sharing Passwords

Your teen needs to understand that their passwords are the keys to their digital houses. By giving someone access to a password, they are giving them the key to see all of their private information: friends, conversations, money transfers via apps, bank accounts, medical history and more. Teach your teen that passwords should be shared in extreme moderation—and always with the best motives.

- Together, you and your teen should come up with passwords that are easy to remember, but difficult to guess.
- Discuss with your teen when and whom it is appropriate to share passwords with and come up with password sharing guidelines like:
  - Share passwords with parents until your high school aged child has demonstrated their maturity while living a life filled with technology and you have good communication.
  - Sometimes share with friends, but only short term, with the intent to change the password immediately after the shared purpose is completed.
  - Share when there is shared management of an account.
  - Never share with a business or online promotion.
  - Use a password manager or notebook to store all your passwords.

Succeeding with Social Media

While it's important to teach your teen about the dangers inherent in their virtual worlds, it's also important to show them what's good about their online interactions, specifically on social media.

1. Ask your teen to describe the greater purposes of social media, as opposed to a place to instigate drama or meet strangers.
2. Encourage your teen to use social media to do what they cannot do easily in their day-to-day lives:
   - Stay connected with people they are not geographically near at the time.
   - Learn about and stay aware of people, interests and opportunities.
   - Improve and further their goals in a positive way.
   - Find positive examples of how social media is used for businesses/public figures and causes.
3. Have your child create a LinkedIn profile to highlight their academic, philanthropic, and/or work related experience.

Spot the fake!

The need for critical thinking extends into the retail arena. Help your teen be able to evaluate purchases before costly mistakes are made!

- Ask your teen to select a product on Amazon and read the reviews. See if you can identify ones that are fake.
- Ask your teen to evaluate sellers on the social media platforms favored by him/her. Select an advertiser. Read the comments in that post and scroll through additional posts looking to see what the comments say. Do a google search on the seller. Ask your teen if this seems like a safe seller to buy from.
- Next time your teen is ready to make an online purchase, ask him/her to read the reviews and use this tool: https://www.fakespot.com/. Then see how the results compare and ask your teen what did they expect to see and if the results surprised them.

Clean Digital Footprint

Ask your teen to take these steps for a social media hygiene:

- Google yourself. Find out what others can learn about you and see if it matches the impression you are hoping to make. You can also setup Google Alerts for your name to get notified when someone posts something about you that is indexed by Google.
- Clean it up. Use the information you gained by Googling yourself and gathered from your social media profiles. Clean up images, updates and comments that don't flatter you or others.
- Lock it down. Now is the time to reconsider privacy settings and with intention be specific about who can and cannot see the details of your private life. But remember, you never know who may be a friend of a friend and be able to see something you thought was a private post.

Chapter 6:
Dive Deeper

Read More And Share What You Learn With Your Child

READ MORE 3rd THROUGH 5th GRADE
- Third Grade Teacher's Brilliant Lesson on Consent Is Going Viral: https://www.parents.com/news/third-grade-teachers-brilliant-lesson-on-consent-is-going-viral/
- Table Talk: Viral Video Shows The Reality of Online Stranger Danger: https://mamabearapp.com/online-stranger-danger/
- Paedophiles 'hunting' children through TikTok app as disturbing messages revealed: https://www.mirror.co.uk/news/uk-news/paedophiles-hunting-children-through-tiktok-14042405
- The Minefield of Talking With Your Children About Sexting: https://www.wsj.com/articles/the-minefield-of-talking-with-your-children-about-sexting-1540047600
- Billie Eilish says watching porn from age 11 'really destroyed my brain': https://www.cnn.com/2021/12/15/entertainment/billie-eilish-porn-scli-intl/index.html

READ MORE 6th THROUGH 8th GRADE:
- Disturbing cyber-bullying statistics ranks SA tops: https://www.iol.co.za/dailynews/news/kwazulu-natal/disturbing-cyber-bullying-statistics-ranks-sa-tops-19493296
- Cyberbullies are fueling suicide: https://www.iol.co.za/saturday-star/news/cyberbullies-are-fuelling-suicide-19459795
- Nicole Lovell murder: Was a Virginia teen lured to her death through a smartphone app?: https://www.cbsnews.com/news/nicole-lovell-murder-was-a-virginia-teen-lured-to-her-death-through-a-smartphone-app/

- North Carolina man posed as 15-year-old on Snapchat to get girls photos: https://www.mypanhandle.com/news/local-news/police-north-carolina-man-posed-as-15-year-old-on-snapchat-to-get-girls-photos/
- 'I have a naked picture of you on my phone' | Once you send it, you don't have control over where it goes: https://www.wusa9.com/article/news/i-have-a-naked-picture-of-you-on-my-phone-once-you-send-it-you-dont-have-control-over-where-it-goes/65-d42091f4-2f85-4e73-93df-6148aecf2f98

READ MORE 9th THROUGH 12th GRADE:

- Talking Consent - Tea Consent: https://www.youtube.com/watch?v=oQbei5JGiT8
- How to Talk to Your Teen About Sexting: https://lifestyle.howstuffworks.com/family/parenting/tweens-teens/how-to-talk-to-teen-about-sexting.htm
- Court docs: Student sexting group uncovered in Fairfax County: http://www.fox5dc.com/news/local-news/court-docs-student-sexting-group-uncovered-in-fairfax-county
- How Jamie went 'from Snapchat hello to rape in five days': https://www.theage.com.au/national/victoria/i-have-made-a-new-friend-how-jamie-went-from-snapchat-hello-to-rape-in-five-days-20210421-p57l9j.html

SAVVY CYBER KIDS RESOURCES:

Want more articles like the above sent to you for free each week? The Savvy Cyber Kids News Feed (https://savvycyberkids.org/tech-talk/savvy-cyber-kids-news-feed/) gathers both the good and the bad news about cyber safety and cyber ethic issues from across the globe, in a weekly email of the headlines and links. Use these articles as conversation starters with your kids.

LEARN MORE AT:
SAVVYCYBERKIDS.ORG

Made in the USA
Columbia, SC
25 August 2022